*O*XFOR
INSPIRED IMAG

The Radcliffe Camera at sunrise

Yet o ye spires of Oxford, domes and towers!
Gardens and groves, your presence overpowers
The soberness of reason.

Wm. Wordsworth – Oxford

*O*XFORD

INSPIRED IMAGES

The Radcliffe Square and the University Church of St Mary the Virgin

JON DAVISON

To Nic , without whom . . . .

This book was printed on Primagloss 330 g/sm for the cover and Primagloss 170 g/sm Ref. 110 for the text pages. Manufactured by A/S De Forenede Papierfabrikker of Denmark at their Dalum paper mill in Odense, supplied by Paper People, from Shepton Mallet in Somerset.

Printed in the U.K. by the KNP Group, Redditch, using a Heidelberg Speedmaster.
Bound in the U.K. by Paperback Binders of Abingdon, Oxon.
Colour Origination by Oxford Litho Plates Limited, of Oxford, using a Crosfield 635/S scanner.
E6 Processing by Joey of Colourbox, Oxford.

Concept Design and Production: Jon Davison
Publishing Consultant: Ricky Capanni
Design Consultant: Mark Hargreaves
Cover Design: Adele Simkin
Typesetting: V.A.P. Publishing Services, Langford Lane, Kidlington, Oxford
Finished Layouts by Terry Aldridge
Quotations compiled by: Miles Chetwynd-Stapylton & Jon Davison
Text: Miles Chetwynd-Stapylton & Tim Davies
Text Editing: Tim Davies
Proof Reading: Nicola Davison
Financial and marketing support: Thames and Chilterns Tourist Board.
All Photographs by Jon Davison except:
Tim Davies: page 65 & page 32 (inset)
Steve Foote: page 47 (bottom right)
Becci Morris: page 80

ISBN 1 869824 00 8

Published by
Jon Davison Communications, P.O. Box 187, Oxford, OX4 1JN, United Kingdom. 0865 250297
© *Jon Davison 1987*

Fellows Brasserie in St Clements

Oxford is on the whole more attractive than Cambridge to the ordinary visitor; and the traveller is therefore recommended to visit Cambridge first, or to omit it altogether if he cannot visit both.

Baedeker's Great Britain (1887), 30. *From London to Oxford*

F O R E W O R D

Blenheim Palace.

September, 1986

Many photographic books of Oxford have appeared over the years, but sadly it seems, very few have come close to evoking its special sense of time and place.

At Blenheim Palace, we have an ideal opportunity to observe the reactions and enjoyment of the many visiting tourists who come here each year.

I feel that 'Inspired Images' comes very close to portraying this enigmatic feeling that Oxford evokes. I have had a certain amount to do with that city over the years and feel that I know something of its 'essence': what I have seen in these images is how I would like to remember Oxford. I would feel proud to offer this book to visitors, to evoke an image and provide a memento.

Marlborough

His Grace the Duke of Marlborough

Blenheim Palace from the Grand Bridge

'Randolph said with pardonable pride, "This is the finest view in England."
Looking at the lake, the bridge, the miles of magnificent park studded with
old oaks . . . and the huge and stately palace, I confess I felt awed. But my
American pride forbade the admission.'

Lady Randolph Churchill

The Radcliffe Camera 3.00 a.m.

INTRODUCTION

Oxford is a name which conjures up many images, to some it is just the home of Morris Motors, to others it evokes more romantic images of spires emerging from morning mists, of May Balls, and of crowds thronging the banks of the Isis, cheering their college eights to victory in the spring 'bumps'.

The name Oxford, which conjures up these diverse images and which has today found a special place in the hearts and minds of millions of people the world over, stems from the city's humble beginnings – quite simply it was the place where oxen crossed a ford in the river. The University, with its customs, architectural beauty, and historical significance (and for which the city is probably best known), did not come into existence until the 13th century (by which time Oxford was a fairly large town), when because of unrest between England and France, those well-heeled young men who had previously crossed the English Channel to be educated in Paris were banned from making such a journey, and for reasons that are not wholly clear (although providence may have played its part) decided to congregate in Oxford.

The history of Oxford is itself an extensive and intriguing tale, but not one that we can do justice to in a book such as this. For this is a book of images, the intention being to allow you, the reader/viewer, the opportunity to see Oxford in a manner that befits its romantic and dreamlike status. For if viewed in a particular way, the picturesque beauty that people have come to associate with Oxford, and which has inspired so many and so much, is there to be seen.

ABOVE: *The Bell Tower of Magdalen College.*
OPPOSITE: *The 'Bridge of Sighs', linking the two halves of Hertford College.*

But let my due feet never fail
To walk the studious cloisters pale
And love the high embowed roof
With antique pillars massive proof,
And storied windows richly dight
Casting a dim religious light.

Milton – 11 Pensero

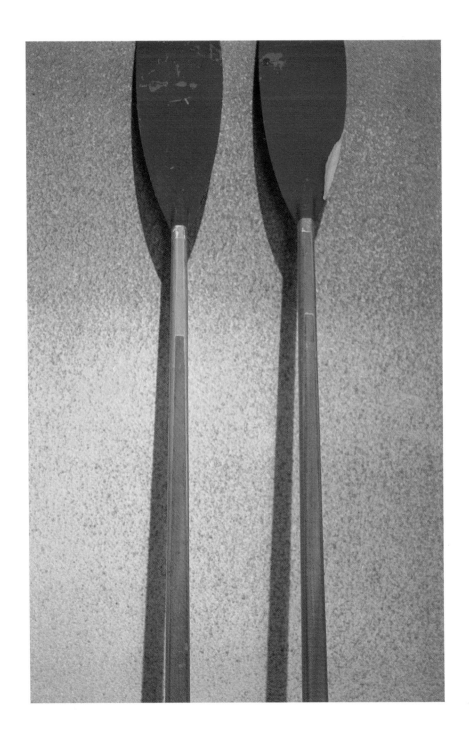

The whole place gives me a deeper sense of English life than anything yet. As I walked along the river I saw hundreds of the mighty lads of England, clad in white flannel and blue, immense, fair-haired, magnificent in their youth, lounging down the stream in their punts or pulling in straining crews and rejoicing in their Godlike strength.

Henry James, in a letter to William James 1869

'Eights Week', the annual inter-college rowing event.

ABOVE: *Autumn in Turl Street.*

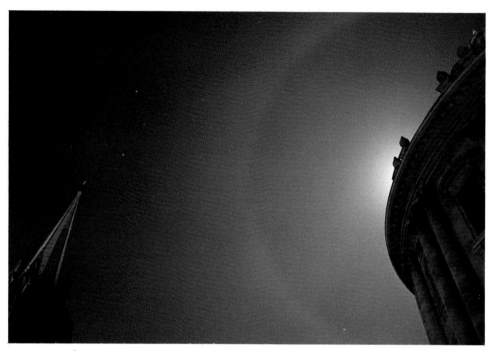

The Moon's refraction through ice particles in the lower stratosphere, over the Radcliffe Square.

And n'er hath city, since a moon began
to hallow nature for the soul of man,
steeped in the freshness of her fairy light,
more richly shone, than Oxford shines tonight.

Robert Montgomery – Oxford 1831

TOP: *Shop window in the High Street.* BOTTOM: *Parks Road.*

The Bodliean Library

Of the Bodliean:
Were I not a king, I would be a University man; and if it were that I must be a prisoner, if I might have my wish, I would have no other prison than this library, and be chained together with these good authors.

James I (Quoted in Rex Platonicus)

ABOVE: *The old city wall at New College.* RIGHT: *Christchurch Cathedral.*

6.00 a.m. .... After the Ball.

Sir, you have tasted two whole worms; you have hissed all your mystery lectures and been caught fighting a liar in the quad; you will leave Oxford by the next town drain.

Attributed to Rev. W. A. Spooner

Sunrise. . . . .

An Hour before the worshipped sun
peered forth the golden window of the east,
a troubled mind drove me to walk abroad.

Shakespeare

OPPOSITE: *The 'Not the Moulin Rouge' cinema, in New High Street, Headington.* ABOVE: *'Untitled', 1986, in New High Street.* LEFT: *The Penultimate Picture Palace, in East Oxford.*

England is the paradise of individuality, eccentricities, anomalies, hobbies, and humours.

George Santayana – The British Character

LEFT & OPPOSITE: *The Radcliffe Camera.* ABOVE: *All Souls and Radcliffe Square.*

The morning after . . . .
OVERLEAF: *The Cricket Pavilion in the University Parks.*

If you feel that you have both feet planted on the ground then the University has failed you.

Robert Cohen — Time June 1961

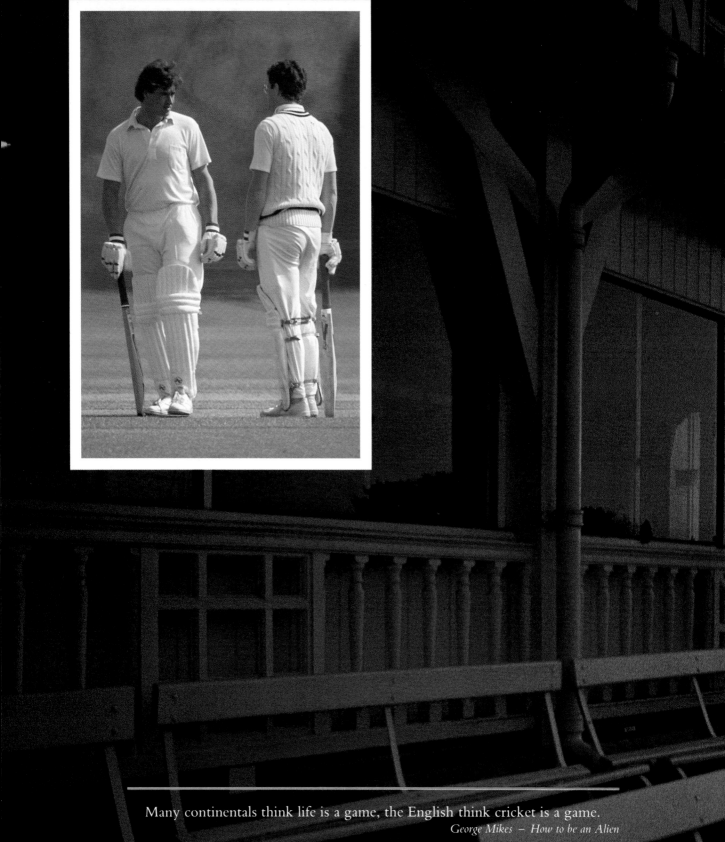

Many continentals think life is a game, the English think cricket is a game.

George Mikes – How to be an Alien

ABOVE & LEFT: *The Oxford Canal.* OPPOSITE: *The Spire of Nuffield College, and the Norman Castle Mound.*

When you have wearied of the valiant spires of this country town,
Of its white streets and glistening museums, and black monastic walls,
Of its red motors and lumbering trams, and self-sufficient people,
I will take you walking with me to a place you have not seen –
Half town and half country, the land of the canal.
It is dearer to me than the antique town: I love it more than the rounded hills:
Straightest and sublimest of rivers is the long canal.

James Elroy Flecker — Oxford Canal

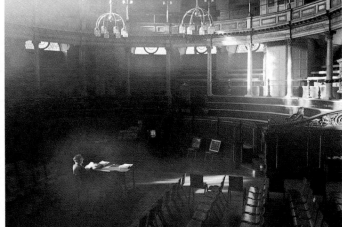

The Sheldonian Theatre.

The River Cherwell, with the Tropical and Sub-Tropical Glasshouses of the Botanical Gardens, from Magdalen Bridge.

ABOVE: *Magdalen Bridge from the Cherwell.*

ABOVE: *The Rover PLC car assembly plant at Cowley.* TOP: *The Lucy Company's Eagle Ironworks, at Jericho.*

Two men look out through the same bars;
One sees the mud, and one the stars

Frank Langbridge – Cluster of quiet thoughts

The Wrought Iron Pillars of the University Museum in Parks Road.

ABOVE: *The Sheldonian Theatre from New College Lane.* OPPOSITE TOP: *Icicles in Catte Street.* OPPOSITE BELOW: *View towards Carfax, from St Mary's.*

There's a certain slant of light
on winter afternoons,
that oppresses like the weight
of cathedral tunes.

Emily Dickinson

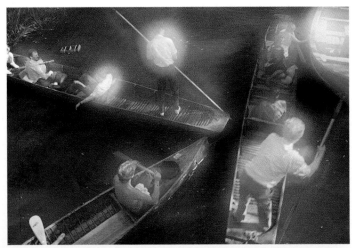

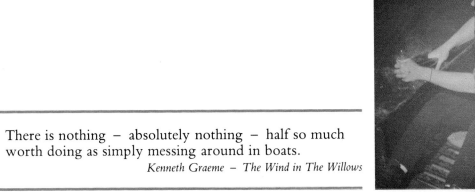

There is nothing – absolutely nothing – half so much worth doing as simply messing around in boats.

Kenneth Graeme – The Wind in The Willows

ABOVE & OPPOSITE: *Tom Tower, Christchurch*

ABOVE *Magdalen College Cloisters and Quad.* OPPOSITE: *Magdalen from the High Street*

There once was at Magdalen Hall
A man who knew nothing at all
He took his degree
At seventy-three
Which is youngish, for Magdalen Hall.

Anon

May morning, The High Street . . . . 6.00 a.m.

We came to Oxford, a mighty fine place and well seated, and cheap
entertainment.

Pepys 9 June 1668

The Nuclear Science and Mechanical Engineering Buildings, on the Banbury Road.

The Clarendon Centre Shopping Arcade.

The Oxford Ice Rink in Oxpens Road.

Exeter College from Ship Street.

Balliol College from Broad Street.

Oh Oxford, thou art lovely still,
For, ever round thy classic towers
Fond Nature with her utmost skill
    The richest gems upon thee showers,
Mid verdure bright on every hand
    Thy Colleges and Churches stand

Henry W. Taunt

. *St Clements from the Plain.*

Cornmarket Street from Ship Street.

It is such a bewildered, scared feeling to go for the first time to a place and not know where to call out to the driver to stop.

Katherine Butler Hathaway

. . . Yet have I seen no place, by inland brook,
Hill-top or plain, or trim arcaded bowers,
That carries age so nobly in its look
As Oxford with the sun upon her towers.

Frederick W. Faber

The Radcliffe Camera and St Mary's Church, from Brasenose College, 6.00 a.m.

Hertford College.

We called him tortoise because he taught us.
C. L. Dodgeson (Lewis Carroll)

The Radcliffe Camera from All Souls College.

The City Skyline from Marston Road.

Park End Street.

The ruins of Godstow Nunnery near Wolvercote.

Magdalen College Chapel.

'Magdalen Walks'.

The Mercury Fountain at Christchurch.

When the High Lama asked him whether Shangri-la was not unique in his experience, and if the Western World could offer anything in the least like it, he answered with a smile: well, yes — to be quite frank, it reminds me very slightly of Oxford.

James Hilton — Lost Horizon

All Souls College.

ABOVE: *The Church of St Mary the Virgin, from Radcliffe Square.* TOP: *The Radcliffe Camera from St Mary's.*

The City Skyline from South Park.

That sweet city with her dreaming spires.
Matthew Arnold – Thyrsis

ABOVE: *The Randolph Hotel, Beaumont Street.*

Very nice sort of place Oxford, I should think, for people who like that sort of place.
George Bernard Shaw – Man and Superman

ABOVE: *Winter training on the Isis.*

71

The Hall at Christchurch.

'The line of festal light in Christchurch Hall'.

Matthew Arnold

Christchurch from Deadman's Walk.

ABOVE: *The Oxford Canal.* ABOVE RIGHT: *The University Museum.* OPPOSITE: *Cyclists in Turl Street.* OPPOSITE RIGHT: *The Norman Castle from Paradise Street.*

ABOVE: *The Eagle and Child in St Giles.*
LEFT: *The Bulldog in St Aldates.*
OPPOSITE: *The Bear in Blue Boar Street.*

There is nothing which has yet been continued by man, by which so much happiness is produced as by a good tavern or inn.

Samuel Johnson

The City Skyline from Marston Road.

'Quality is what ultimately counts; this is what Oxford always stood for,
and will either stand   by − or fall − in what future there may be for us'.

A. L. Rowse
from: OXFORD, in the History of a Nation

Ashmolean Museum in Beaumont Street

ACKNOWLEDGEMENTS

This book has gone through many changes and the final product, that you see in front of you, owes a great deal to many people.

I would like to extend special thanks to Chris Fone and Ricky Capanni, for without their help, advice, and understanding of the world of Publishing, and their unique knowledge of the Public Houses of Great Britain (most notably where to find them), this book would never have been completed . . . Hic. Special thanks must also go to Alan Bunting.

Finally, many thanks to those people whose presence and enthusiasm has kept this project alive and well over the past year. Most notably,

Tim Davies	Tony Davies	Peter Alexander
Richard Leonard	Miles Chetwynd-Stapylton	Paul Duffie
Earl Beesley	Dave Hix	Murray Reid
Nick Fogden	Jenny Fox	Tony & JoAn Davies
Mark Hargreaves	Steve Foote	Elinore Fairhurst
Adele Simkin	Donna Bundy	The Staff of the Randolph Hotel

The images in this book were all taken with Fujichrome Transparency film (100 and 3200 ISO). The camera used was a Nikon F3 35mm with lenses ranging from: 28mm Shift, 135mm, 200mm, 1.2 50mm. (Backup was with a Nikon EM, the medium format camera was a Hasselblad 500C.)

The Filters used were: Polarising (for blue enhancement). 80a & 85b and FL Day for colour temperature correction.

No other filters were used and the light has been recorded exactly as it was seen.

All were taken over the last two years, and are part of the Jon Davison Stock Image Library, which specialises in the leasing of contemporary colour transparencies for publication or display.

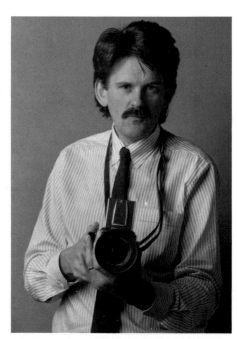

Jon Davison was born in Auckland, New Zealand in 1950. He moved to Australia in 1973, where he worked as a freelance photographer, primarily for Television and Film. Jon came to England in 1980 and settled in Oxford where, over the past seven years, he has built up a reputation as one of the city's most gifted and respected photographers.

Jon Davison by Becci Morris.